by Ellen Lawrence

Consultants:

Suzy Gazlay, MA
Recipient, Presidential Award for Excellence in Science Teaching

Kimberly Brenneman, PhD
National Institute for Early Education Research, Rutgers University, New Brunswick, New Jersey

BEARPORT
PUBLISHING

New York, New York

Credits

Cover © Robert Neumann/Shutterstock; 3, © CoraMax/Shutterstock, © Vitaly Korovin/Shutterstock, and © FocalPoint/Shutterstock; 4-5, © gkuna/Shutterstock, © Cultura Limited/Superstock, © Juniors/Superstock, © Artex67/Shutterstock, © Joshua Rainey Photography/Shutterstock, © RusGri/Shutterstock, © Alis Photo/Shutterstock, © irin-k/Shutterstock, © arka 38/Shutterstock, and © Coramax/Shutterstock; 6-7, © Coramax/Shutterstock and © Ruby Tuesday Books; 8-9, © Coramax/Shutterstock, © anaken 2012/Shutterstock, © Dino Osmic/Shutterstock, © Maen CG/Shutterstock, and © Pixelspieler/Shutterstock; 10-11, © Coramax/Shutterstock and © Ruby Tuesday Books; 12-13, © Coramax/Shutterstock and © Ruby Tuesday Books; 14-15, © Coramax/Shutterstock, © Ruby Tuesday Books, © FocalPoint/Shutterstock, and © Vitaly Korovin/Shutterstock; 16-17, © Richard Griffin/Shutterstock, © Coramax/Shutterstock, © Imageman/Shutterstock, © titov dmitriy/Shutterstock, © xpixel/Shutterstock, © Lubava/Shutterstock, © Vitaly Korovin/Shutterstock, © Ruby Tuesday Books, © Madlen/Shutterstock, and © Richard Griffin/Shutterstock; 18-19, © Coramax/Shutterstock, © SeDmi/Shutterstock, © Tsekhmister/Shutterstock, © Madlen/Shutterstock, © Jacob Kearns/Shutterstock, and © Ruby Tuesday Books; 20-21, © Coramax/Shutterstock, © Ruby Tuesday Books, © Mayovskyy Andrew/Shutterstock, © arka 38/Shutterstock, © Madlen/Shutterstock, and © Richard Griffin/Shutterstock; 22, © Rob Marmion/Shutterstock, © Olga Miltsova/Shutterstock, © oksix/Shutterstock, © Wildnerdpix/Shutterstock, and © Monkey Business Images/Shutterstock; 23, © Siim Sepp/Wikipedia Creative Commons, © Georgy Markov/Shutterstock, © Richard Griffin/Shutterstock, and © daseaford/Shutterstock.

Publisher: Kenn Goin
Editorial Director: Adam Siegel
Creative Director: Spencer Brinker
Design: Emma Randall
Photo Researcher: Ruby Tuesday Books Ltd.

Library of Congress Cataloging-in-Publication Data in process at time of publication (2013)
Library of Congress Control Number: 2012046349
ISBN-13: 978-1-61772-737-5 (library binding)

For more information, write to Bearport Publishing Company, Inc., 45 West 21st Street, Suite 3B, New York, New York 10010. Printed in the United States of America.

10 9 8 7 6 5 4 3 2 1

Contents

Let's Investigate Soil

It can be black or brown, crumbly or sticky, and often very messy.
Sometimes people call it dirt or mud, but its real name is soil.
You probably see soil every day in gardens or at the park.
Now it's time to look at soil like a scientist. Inside this book are
lots of fun experiments and cool facts about this amazing stuff.
So grab your notebook, and let's start investigating soil!

Check It Out!

In your notebook, make a list of all the places you see soil.

- Describe what the soil looks like.
- Are there plants growing in it?
- What do you think soil is made of?

Be a Good Scientist

- Always get permission from a grown-up before digging up soil from a yard or garden.
- Be sure to wash your hands with soap and warm water after touching soil.

What is soil made of?

All soil is not the same. For example, the soil in one place might feel soft and crumbly, while in another area it may be hard as a rock. Soil can also be red, brown, or even gray. So why is soil different from place to place? Let's begin our investigation by finding out what makes up soil.

You will need:

- Soil from a place where plants are growing
- A small, clear jar with a screw-top lid
- A notebook and pencil
- Water
- A magnifying glass

1 Place two inches (5 cm) of soil into a jar. In your notebook, write a description of the soil.

▶ What color is it?

▶ How does it look and feel? For example, is it crumbly and light like sand, or sticky and lumpy like thick oatmeal?

Write down your observations.

Add water to the jar until it is about three-quarters full.

 After an hour, use a magnifying glass to observe the contents of the jar.

Screw the lid tightly on the jar. Then shake the jar for 30 seconds.

In your notebook, record what you see.

▶ What is floating on top of the water?

▶ What do you see at the bottom of the jar?

Make a list of the **ingredients** in the soil.

▶ How do you think these ingredients got into the soil?

(To learn more about this investigation and find the answers to the questions, see pages 20–21.)

How do rocks become soil?

Soil is mainly made up of tiny **grains**, or pieces, of rock. There are many different ways in which solid rock gets broken into tiny pieces. For example, rocks in rivers get smashed against each other by fast-moving water. Wind and rain also wear away the surface of rocks, making small pieces fall off. All these tiny grains of rock collect on the ground and become soil over thousands of years. Let's investigate how this happens.

You will need:

- Ten stones or small pieces of rock
- A metal container with a lid, such as a coffee can
- A pitcher of water
- A notebook and pencil
- A coffee filter

1 Collect ten stones or pieces of rock. Try to find different kinds.

2 Put the stones in a metal container and then pour in enough water to cover the stones. Make sure the container's lid is on tight!

Shake the container 1,000 times! You don't have to do this all at once, or even on the same day. Try splitting the shakes into 10 groups of 100. Ask friends or family members to help out.

▶ **What do you think will happen to the stones?**

Write down your **prediction** in your notebook.

 After shaking the container 1,000 times, remove the stones from the water.

 Ask someone to hold a coffee filter over a sink. Slowly pour the water from the container into the filter.

▶ **What do you observe in the coffee filter?**

In your notebook, write down what you think has happened.

▶ **Does your prediction match what happened?**

(To learn more about this investigation and find the answers to the questions, see pages 20–21.)

9

Are dead plants in soil?

Tiny grains of rock are the main ingredient in soil. However, dead plants are also an important part of soil. When you put garden soil in a jar of water, did you notice tiny bits of leaves, twigs, or **roots** floating in the water? When plants die or leaves fall from trees, they lay on the ground. The plant material begins to **rot** and gets mixed into the soil. It may take several months, but eventually the plant material gets **moldy** and crumbly and becomes part of the soil. Let's investigate how this happens.

You will need:

- Leaves, grass clippings, or fruit and vegetable peelings
- A string fruit or vegetable bag
- A piece of string about 20 inches (51 cm) long
- A small rock
- A small shovel
- A small area of soil in a garden, or a container filled with potting soil
- A cup of water
- A notebook and pencil

 Put leaves, grass, and other plant material into a string bag.

 Tie one end of a string to the bag and tie the other end around a small rock.

Use a shovel to dig a hole about ten inches (25 cm) deep in soil, or in a container of potting soil. Put the bag into the hole. Pour a cup of water over the bag. If the plant material is wet, it will rot faster.

 In your notebook, write down the date and then describe the plant material that you buried.

Once a week for one month, dig up the bag and examine its contents. Then pour a cup of water over the bag and bury it again.

Each week, keep a journal of what you observe.

▶ What does the plant material look like?

▶ How is it different from the week before?

▶ How is it the same?

 Cover the bag with soil, making sure the end of the string and the rock are not buried. Place the rock on the surface to mark the spot where you buried the bag.

(To learn more about this investigation and find the answers to the questions, see pages 20–21.)

11

What is in a cup of soil?

Soil is made up of tiny pieces of rock and dead plants, but what else is in soil? It's hard to imagine, but just one cup of soil can be home to millions of living things. Some, like beetles or worms, are big enough to see. Others, however, are so tiny we cannot see them. Let's investigate what is in a cup of soil.

You will need:

- A cup of soil from a place where plants are growing
- Four sheets of white paper
- A magnifying glass
- A toothpick or teaspoon
- Tweezers
- A jar
- A notebook and pencil

1 Empty a cup of soil onto a sheet of white paper.

 Look closely at the soil with a magnifying glass. Use a toothpick or a spoon to spread out the soil to see what items are in it.

Separate the things you find into three sets:

- Nonliving: for example, grains of rocks or stones
- Once-living: plant material or dead insects
- Living: animals such as worms, beetles, or ants

Use tweezers to place the nonliving and once-living items onto two separate sheets of paper.

nonliving

once-living

If you see a living thing, such as an insect or worm, carefully pick it up with your fingers and put it into a jar.

 In your notebook, list all the things you find in the soil. For example:

Nonliving	Once-living	Living
grains of sand	small twig	worm
brown pebble	roots	ant
two white pebbles	pieces of a dead leaf	round seeds
brown grains of rock		

 When you have finished your investigation, put the animals and soil back outside.

(To learn more about this investigation and find the answers to the questions, see pages 20–21.)

Which type of soil holds water best?

Most plants live in soil and need water to grow and be healthy. They use their roots to take in water from soil. When it rains, water collects in tiny spaces in the soil called pores. Some types of soil have lots of pores that hold water. Other types of soil do not. Plants grow best in soil that holds plenty of water. In this experiment, you will test different soils to find out which one holds water the best.

 Collect three different types of soil. Fill each flowerpot with one type.

You will need:

- Three different types of soil (the soil must be dry)
- Three flowerpots with holes in the bottom
- A black marker
- A notebook and pencil
- Three bowls
- A measuring cup
- Water

soil from an area where plants don't grow

soil from a garden or yard where plants are growing

potting soil from a garden center

Use a marker to label the pots.

potting soil

▸ Which type of soil do you think will hold the most water? Why?

▸ Which will hold the least? Why?

Write your predictions and ideas in your notebook.

Place each pot in a bowl and then slowly pour a cup of water into each flowerpot. Any water the soil can't hold will run out into the bowl.

After 30 minutes, check the bowls. Measure how much water is in each bowl by pouring it into a measuring cup.

In your notebook, record the amount of water in each bowl.

▸ Which flowerpot had the least amount of water in its bowl?

That type of soil held the most water.

▸ Why do you think that is? Do your predictions about which types of soil hold the most and least water match what happened?

▸ Compare the soils that held the most and the least water. How are they different?

(To learn more about this investigation and find the answers to the questions, see pages 20–21.)

Which type of soil is best for growing plants?

In order to grow and be healthy, plants need substances called **nutrients**. Plants take in nutrients from soil through their roots. Most plants grow best in soil with lots of nutrients. Let's investigate which type of soil is best for growing bean plants.

roots

1 Collect four different types of soil. For example:

Soil 1: potting soil from a garden center

Soil 2: soil from a garden or yard where plants are growing

Soil 3: soil from an area where plants don't grow

Soil 4: potting soil mixed with sand

You will need:

- Four different types of soil
- Four flowerpots and saucers
- A black marker
- Bean seeds
- A notebook and pencil

2 Fill each flowerpot nearly to the top with one type of soil. Use a marker to label each pot.

garden soil

3 Place two bean seeds in each pot.

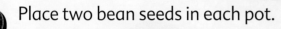

Cover the seeds with soil, then press down gently.

▶ In which soil do you think the plants will grow best? Why?

Write your predictions in your notebook.

4 Stand each pot in a saucer and then place the pots in front of a sunny window. Water the pots to keep the soil moist. Give each pot the same amount of water.

As the bean plants grow, record in your notebook what happens.

▶ Which plant grows the fastest? Which one looks healthiest?

▶ Which type of soil is best for growing bean plants? Why?

▶ Do your predictions match what happened?

(To learn more about this investigation and find the answers to the questions, see pages 20–21.)

How do worms help plants?

Earthworms eat dead plants and soil. The plants and soil are broken down inside the worm's body and then released back into the soil as poop. Worm poop contains lots of nutrients that plants need. Let's make a worm garden and investigate the secret underground world of worms.

You will need:

- An empty two-liter soda bottle
- Duct tape
- Gravel or stones
- Garden soil
- Sand
- Half a cup of water
- Five small worms (Look for worms in soil where plants are growing.)
- Pieces of dead leaves, grass clippings, or other plant material
- A notebook and pencil
- A plate
- A dark cloth

1 Ask an adult to cut off the top of a plastic soda bottle and make six pea-sized holes in the bottom. Tape over any sharp edges at the top of the bottle using duct tape.

cut here

make holes here

worm food

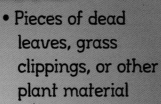
worms

2 Put about two inches (5 cm) of gravel or stones in the bottle. Then add layers of soil and sand. Pour half a cup of water into the bottle.

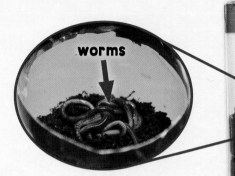

worms

soil

sand

soil

sand

soil

stones

3 Place five worms on the top layer of soil in the bottle. Cover them with about one inch (2.5 cm) of plant material.

▶ What do you think the worms will do?

▶ What will happen to the plant material?

Write down your predictions in your notebook.

4 Stand the worm garden on a plate in case any water leaks out. Place it somewhere cool and cover it with a dark cloth.

After three days, check the worm garden. In your notebook, write down what you observe.

▶ What is happening to the plant material?

▶ What do you notice about the layers of sand and soil?

▶ Do your predictions match what happened?

5 Check on your garden every few days. In your notebook, note any changes you observe. If the soil looks dry, add half a cup of water. Give the worms more plant material to eat, too. After two weeks, put your worms back where you found them.

(To learn more about this investigation and find the answers to the questions, see pages 20–21.)

Discovery Time

It's fun to investigate the world using science. Now let's check out all the amazing things we discovered about soil.

What is soil made of?

Pages 6-7

Soil is made up of tiny pieces of broken rock. Did you see small grains of rock at the bottom of your jar?

Most soil also contains pieces of plants, such as twigs, seeds, and dead leaves and flowers. Did you see tiny pieces of plants floating in the water in your jar?

Soil looks different from place to place because it's made up of different types of rock. It also contains different amounts of plant material.

plant pieces

rock grains

How do rocks become soil?

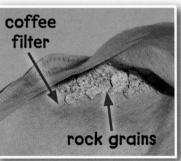

coffee filter

rock grains

Pages 8-9

When you shook the container, the small rocks and stones in the water smashed against each other, causing tiny grains of rock to break off.

Grains of rock, like the ones in the coffee filter, are the main ingredient of soil. Just like the rocks in the container of water, rocks in rivers often get smashed together. The grains of rock that break off sink to the bottom of the river and become soil.

Are dead plants in soil?

Pages 10-11

The plant material in the bag will slowly rot.

It may break apart or become moldy.

This happens because millions of tiny living things in the soil are breaking down the plant material.

Then it becomes part of the soil.

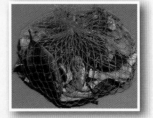

plant material before it is buried

plant material after 4 weeks

What is in a cup of soil?

Every cup of soil you examine will be different. Soil from a garden may contain lots of plant material. This can make the soil feel soft and crumbly. Soil that contains plant matter may be home to many small plant-eating animals, such as worms.

Soil from a place where there are no plants might be mostly made up of grains of rock. This soil might be dry and hard. There may be no animals living in this soil.

Which type of soil holds water best?

Soil that contains lots of dead plant material usually holds more water than soil that is mostly made up of grains of rock. This is because the plant material helps to create pores where water can collect.

Which type of soil is best for growing plants?

Soil that is made up of lots of dead plant material usually contains lots of nutrients. As a result, most plants grow best in this type of soil.

How do worms help plants?

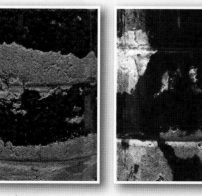

day 1   day 14

Worms eat dead plant material. Then they help living plants by releasing nutrients into the soil in their poop.

When worms move around underground, they mix and break up the soil. This makes spaces where water can collect. So worms help soil to hold the water that plants need to grow.

21

Soil in Action

You might not have paid much attention to soil before. Now that you've discovered so much about this amazing stuff, keep an eye out to see what is happening to soil in the world around you!

1. Look at the grass on a football or soccer field.

▶ **What do you think is beneath the grass?**

2. In the fall, the leaves of many trees in gardens, parks, and forests fall to the ground.

▶ **What do you think might happen to these leaves?**

3. When it rains, water falls on soil where plants are growing.

▶ **What do you think happens to the water?**

4. When you are at the beach, you might see waves crashing against the cliffs.

▶ **How do you think the waves will change the cliffs?**

5. Many foods that people eat come from plants. Without soil, these plants couldn't grow.

▶ **What foods have you eaten today that came from plants?**

Answers:
1. Grass grows in soil, so there may be millions of worms and other tiny living things beneath your feet as you play a game of soccer or football. 2. After leaves fall to the ground, they rot and become part of the soil. 3. The rain may trickle into pores, or spaces, in the soil. Then plants take in the water through their roots. 4. Waves that crash against cliffs break off tiny grains of rock that make up sand. 5. Foods such as potatoes, apples, and oranges all come from plants, as well as foods such as bread and cookies that are made from wheat. Without soil, plants couldn't grow.

22

Science Words

grains (GRAYNZ) tiny pieces of something, such as rock or sand

ingredients (in-GREED-ee-uhnts) different parts or substances that make up something; for example, grains of rock and pieces of plants are both ingredients of soil

grains of sand

moldy (MOHLD-ee) covered with a furry growth of tiny living things called fungi that cause once-living things to break down

nutrients (NOO-tree-uhnts) substances in soil that come from dead plants and animals, and which plants need to grow and be healthy

prediction (pri-DIK-shuhn) a guess that something will happen in a certain way; it is often based on facts a person knows or something a person has observed

roots (ROOTS) underground parts of plants that take in water and nutrients from the soil; roots also spread out in the soil to hold a plant in place

roots

rot (ROT) to become soft and moldy and slowly break down into tiny pieces

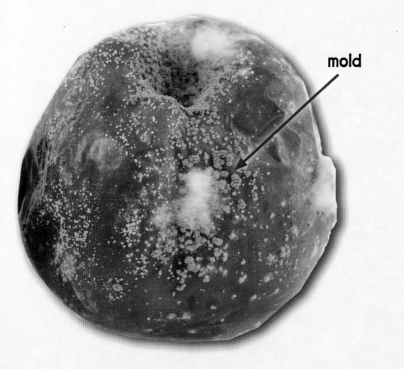

mold

23

Index

Read More

Lunis, Natalie. *Wiggly Earthworms (No Backbone!).* New York: Bearport (2009).

Owen, Ruth. *Science and Craft Projects with Rocks and Soil (Get Crafty Outdoors).* New York: Rosen (2013).

Rosinky, Natalie M. *Dirt: The Scoop on Soil.* Minneapolis, MN: Capstone (2003).

Learn More Online

To learn more about dirt, visit
www.bearportpublishing.com/FundamentalExperiments

About the Author

Ellen Lawrence lives in the United Kingdom. Her favorite books to write are those about nature and animals. In fact, the first book Ellen bought for herself, when she was six years old, was the story of a gorilla named Patty Cake that was born in New York's Central Park Zoo.